ALL OF US

Fabrienne Trebizo

PUBLICATIONS

Published in the United States by
Winn Publications LLC, Texas.

Visit us on the Web!
WinnPublications.com
AllOfUs.Shop

ISBN: 9780578647388
Library of Congress Control Number: 2020934240

DEDICATION

Dedicated to my family.
Honoring my daughters and my sons.
Thank you for allowing me to figure out who I am.
Thank you for sharing your life with me.
To my family and friends
who played a major part in my healing.
I am forever grateful.

TABLE OF CONTENTS

Acknowledgements

About The Author

BETWEEN YOU AND ME

Ever just sit and wonder why things happen in your life the way they do? You sit wonder how you know the knowledge you know. You think about things you have never heard of and how you feel things

you can't even see.

Some may say you're crazy, but I believe you. Sometimes I wonder if anyone else feels the way I do. I feel out of place most of the time. Different from everyone around me including family members. I even get this overwhelming sense of there being something bigger than me. When I was younger, I used to walk everywhere and imagine what my life would be like if I lived in a city. I was raised in a small town- Porterville, California - where there was no city around close by. How did I even know what living in the city would be like? Here in Porterville it's filled with nothing but agriculture. No malls. No high tower buildings. Definitely no flashing lights. Still, I was already yearning for something I knew nothing about. The weight of this desire, this emotion, was heavy for a 12-year-old. Nothing in particular triggered these emotions. I just knew I craved something I couldn't see or touch. I just knew I was meant to do something bigger than me.

I would set intentions out not even knowing what I was tapping into. One time I was so sad. I was missing my dad and I just cried and cried and cried. My mom was getting frustrated because I wouldn't settle down. She tried calling him and couldn't get through, she was just making it worse. Here I was throwing a temper tantrum when I ran to the door to find my dad walking up to the doorstep. Did he hear me cry? Did he feel my pain? Or did I manifest him with my pure hurting heart? Sometimes things just happen in our lives and there's no real explanation for it.

Here I am, now an adult, living on the outskirts of the city. I found myself settling in the City of Angels- Los

Angeles, California. Where the buildings are high rise buildings and the traffic is horrendous. Where on one side of the street you will see homeless, lost spirits, and then on the other you will see brand new BMWs and Teslas. Where the bright lights are vibrant with colors of every shade.

I find myself retreating back to that small town just to have one more glimpse of what was once my home. When I go back it feels right. It feels like I need to stay home. It's so hard to leave. I just want to pick up from where I left off and build from the person I am today. When I get back to the outskirts of the city, it feels right too. I feel independent and ambitious. How do I split myself in half so I can have the best of both worlds?

FEEL THE MUSIC IN YOUR BODY

Ever just sit and listen to music? You really hear the lyrics and wonder if the artist is singing to or for you. You feel it with every inch inside of you.

Sometimes I feel like music is the only thing that could ever understand me. Lyrics seem to sing my thoughts and beats seem to relax my mind. Sometimes it makes me fall so deeply in love with love.

Most of the time I can only express myself with songs. With some lyrics, it seems like I could have written them myself. The beats hit so hard I can almost feel it entered my body. Like a euphoric feeling. Sometimes the beats feel so good and the lyrics are so perfect I get chills in my face.

Music definitely sets the tone for the day. The unforgettable memories that certain songs bring. They can almost take you back to that moment. If it was a good feeling, like a feeling of home, home is there when you close your eyes. Listen in. Music is so powerful. What we put in our ears is what we feed to our spirit.

My favorite is the late-night drives and spontaneous road trips. I have a playlist for each situation. There's something about driving, thinking and playing my music loud. It somehow clears the mind. I think the best while I'm listening to music. I can absorb more information when I have music in the background. My body works out to the beat of the music. My emotions change as the music changes. When I'm cleaning the house, music is blaring. If you visit my home in the evening you will hear three to four different songs playing in the house from all different directions.

I found out when I feel the loneliest, music helps me remember that I'm not alone.

FALLING IN LOVE

Ever just fall in love with love? You ever lose yourself in someone else's love, forget about who you are, then repeat the cycle?

Man, one thing about love is that everyone wants to know it. I mean think about it, we would kill ourselves to feel it. Men would be willing to break their backs for it. Women would give up their souls to have it. Children would act out so that their parents can be reminded that they need it. Babies cry if you don't nurture them with it. Love is so big. It has so many different levels and phases. Do we even really understand how deep love is?

I've always fallen in love with being in love. The first stages of love are so beautiful. The constant communication, the yearning of your persons touch, the softness of your person's lips, the smell they carry that makes you feel safe. The "good mornings" and "sweet dream" messages. All of those emotions of feeling special. Love, it's so powerful.

I fall in love so deep it's almost like an addiction. I lose myself completely in my person. I tell myself all the time to always be prepared for the unknown. Life hasn't been the greatest. But when I love, I love with everything inside of me. I love so hard I get blinded by love conquering all. If the relationship is toxic, I fall in love with trying to fix it. If it's healthy and it feels good, I fall in love with trying to keep it fresh. If it's over, I fall in love with a beautiful farewell.

I remember one time my person and I were going through the breaking up stage. You know where you still kind of see each other just to make sure you're doing the right thing. I met him at the mall in the parking lot. The song "Dangerously In Love" from BeeHive was playing. We must have cried and hugged throughout the whole song. We knew it was really over. Now I can't listen to that song without feeling some type of sadness. I can still feel how tight the embrace was.

Now, If there was only some way we could restore broken love.

WHEN REGRET RESONATES

Ever just sit and let the regret set in? You ever feel it so deep in your stomach that you crawl into a ball and just cry?

Sometimes when I smoke cannabis my emotions intensify. I try and block any negative thoughts that enter my mind but they somehow seep in anyways. I've said something's out of hurt that I've regretted later. I've betrayed someone's trust to prove a point and it cut me deep in karma. I've held onto things I should have let go a long time ago. I've been so stubborn that I've let the ugly part of me take control.

My impulsive decisions have me tattooed all over the place. Each and every step of these occasions I have been in a corner somewhere in my room or in my closet curled into a ball. Crying my eyes out. Alone. Racing thoughts of the "What if's?" or "I should haves," fill my head.

The pounding of the, "Why did I just do that?" The shaming of myself for holding onto something that caused so much damage to myself later on in life. The "You know betters," that I had to knock down one at a time. In my mother's voice, in my father's voice and my grandmother's voice- please make it stop.

One day I just woke up and said, "Shit has to change in order for it to stop." Such a simple answer to all that ongoing chaos, "Change it." Then, of course, the daily stubborn battle of, "Can I change? What's going to happen next? Will I be okay alone?" All these doubts set in and make it nearly emotionally impossible to change the mind frame. If you have ever been there, then you know. We are so tired by the time we have to remember to shift our thought process.

I have learned to train my mind as if I was going to the gym. I've managed to make it a daily goal. When I start feeling scared to be alone, I immediately talk to one of my kids. I start asking for reassurance from them. I remind them how important they are to me in my everyday breathtaking life. When I start feeling lonely, I will reach out and say, "Hey, I could use a hug right now." I used to be embarrassed to request such a simple gesture. When I am reminded of something shameful, I retreat back to my beliefs. I remember I am human. I remember I am built with love and imagination. I am who I am because of all that shame. The trick is you actually have to believe what you're telling yourself in order for it to work.

Once I adjusted to the new mindset. Little by little I started feeling more powerful inside. I learned how to control my emotions or at least attempt to keep my emotions balanced. I started seeing my own faults and it has shown me what I could do to have different outcomes.

Move slow and steady like a turtle.

Sometimes the regret is left after the death of a loved one and honestly, there's nothing that can take that away. When my dad died in 2004, it was traumatic. There was no beautiful goodbye, no opportunity to say anything I wished I could have, no sound... nothing. Nothing but the last fight we got into. The boundaries I was trying to create. The change I was looking for, for the family I wanted. The ultimatum I gave him for something I didn't understand at the time.

Regret can be the death of us if we don't forgive ourselves. Regret can make us physically sick and be a vampire to our souls. I had to reprogram my brain. I have to tell myself daily my dad knows my heart better than I know my own right now. He's the lucky one that no longer lives in this realm. I'm sure he would appreciate the outcome of my life and the lives I have helped create.

My advice if you're struggling with regret: learn to let it go.

ALONE ENOUGH

Ever lay in bed alone wondering if you're good enough, or if you're on someone else's mind or do you even exist?

You know even when you're in a relationship you can still feel alone in the bed. This just doesn't apply to single people. I remember so many nights I would lay in bed with my person and I felt so alone. Some nights were when I was in a marriage and some nights were just by choice.

It feels like you want to be held or you want your back rubbed or even caresses through your hair, and you have someone laying there with you and none of this is even remotely close to your person's thinking process. Not even your somber energy motivates your person to give you any kind of affirmations that you desperately need to hear. Here you are laying with an empty stare gazing into the creases of the wall asking yourself, "Do I even exist to them?"

Life can be so hectic. I get that. We all desire our own individuality. I crave mine every single day. I also believe that when you and your person commit to life promises, one of them is to honor your person. Knowing when to act on your affection is so important. Doing so is a part of honoring your person. The simple secret is to memorize your person's spirit patterns. If you're in love, this should be so easy to do. I can guarantee you're already doing it but don't even know it. If you're not and it becomes a task, then that should sum up where you stand with your part in the relationship. This will help you have a better understanding of how to help your person vibrate higher. It's so important.

There have been so many nights where I had to retreat my mind back to my beliefs. I kept reminding myself that there is a matching vibration spirit somewhere and my person would just know to give me affirmations and affections when I feel like I don't exist. Every heartbreak seemed to be worth the risk of opening up to finding my person.

So many times, I have laid in bed in the dead silent and wondered if I'm on anyone else's mind. Is anyone craving my spirit? My affirmations? Is anyone aching for my caress of their head? If you're anything like me, you're probably having racing thoughts about whether you're good enough to be on someone's mind too. Thinking about all the reasons why you're not.

That saying, "An idle mind is the devil's playground," is spot on. Especially late at night when you're lying in bed feeling so alone. And when you're married it hurts worse. Imagine, just lying there crying or in some cases your mental health has a flare and your person is just lying there watching tv, or on their phone, or in another room, or out with their friends.

Today's relationships don't even stand a chance. Traditions have been altered. The act of honoring your partner has now become a difficult task. The thought of marriage is taken so lightly because of how easy it is to sign divorce papers.

Lying in bed feeling lonely can be very dangerous.

FEELING LONELY CAN LEAD TO A DANGEROUS SITUATION

Ever feel so lonely you start talking to your spirit within? You ever had thoughts start to race and slow down at the same time and the feeling of out of place sets in?

I remember when I was younger, I had to share a room with my mom. I used to lay there pretending I had my own room and the things that were on the wall were mine. The stacks of nail polishes and all the clothes in the closet, they were mine too. None of that was even close to the truth. When there wasn't enough room to sleep with my mom I would climb into my grandma's bed. Talk about a lonely child.

There would be days I would walk to and from school or to a friend's house close by and I would have all these racing thoughts and visions. I mean I would actually feel the presence of someone or someplace. When my mind crossed something intriguing it would slow down. Almost like a slow-motion media clip.

I knew if I told someone about all these mental conversations and astroplaning I was doing back then, I don't think I would have been taken seriously. I kept a lot inside. It was so lonely not to be able to share these things with anyone. I'm from a small town with not much to do but to think. When it was dark outside, I would stare at the stars. Every time I looked up my spirit knew there was something bigger than all of us out there.

I used to have these recurring dreams when I was younger. It was almost like a nightmare. In my dream, I was laying down and all these faces were coming at me. All different shades and smiles. All different facial structures and teeth shapes. They just kept getting closer and closer to me. I would wake up every time sweating and the heavy presence of not being alone would still be lingering.

It was then that I started realizing that I didn't fit in. I was who I was on the outside, but my spirit was something completely different on the inside. I was always ahead of myself, real mature for my age which got me into trouble. I didn't have many friends but a handful. I was so naive in love and life growing up. I thought love was liberating. I was in a whole different realm than my peers.

Throughout my early pre-teens I started writing stories, poetry, songs and anything that I could create with words. My racing thoughts were still in full effect. Sometimes I couldn't even get the words out fast enough. Sometimes friends would ask me to write poetry for them. It was my outlet. All these overwhelming emotions of a lonely little girl.

By the time I was able to embrace this gift, I was already trying to end my life. I felt so conflicted about things I saw and was going through that I didn't understand. I knew I was always sad, and I was always searching for something.

Lonely can be a dangerous emotion if it's not handled

correctly. At the end of the day even though we may feel lonely and no one is there to listen or bounce perspectives with, remember this, if you close your eyes and embrace the silence you will hear your spirit tell you it's ok. Almost as soft as a whisper.

DON'T LET ANGER TAKE OVER

Ever feel so angry you catch yourself screaming at the top of your lungs, breaking material things that don't even matter, and hateful

words start to spill from your lips?

Heads up to whosoever in the way when chairs are being thrown in the air. I'm pushing so many buttons before I completely walk away from any relationship. When I say relationship, I don't only mean romantic ones, I mean any type of relationship. They could be my friends, family, or lovers and I could still walk out of their life.

I'm not so confrontational with my person. I'm more passive-aggressive. It takes me a bit to walk away. To be able to say I've screamed at the top of my lungs, it really had to take a lot of my own buttons to be pushed to get there. I hate being lied to. Trust is such a fragile thing. It really does take years to build and seconds to lose. I hate being disrespected and then it makes it worse when my person tries to manipulate the situation by treating me as if I'm naive or my eyes have deceived me.

Screaming at the top of my lungs because I'm so angry. Regretting it the next day because I gave all my power away. Notice how when you're arguing with someone or you're crying, and you get so tired. It's because we give up all of our energy to that person.

I had to learn how to discipline my emotions. It was so hard to do. My impulsive reaction always wants to lash out, say mean things, or even calling someone's phone like crazy. Ever since I figured out that I was giving up my spiritual powers when I allowed myself to be consumed by all the negative emotions, I made it a point to learn how to discipline my emotions even more. It's very liberating and very important to learn this gift.

I had to learn how to align my chakras. It sounds simple, but it's not. Once you start tapping into that part of life, your life will completely change. It will feel like a torna-do hit you. You may find love or maybe get a divorce. You may be rich then be completely broke. You may be homeless and then end up with a life-changing opportu-nity.

You will definitely know when you're ready for that change.

HAPPINESS

Ever feel so happy, you get chills down your spine? It's almost like the feeling of being caressed down your lower back which makes your

body arch.

I know, it sounds euphoric, doesn't it? It's almost a similar feeling. Sometimes I will be driving, and I feel so uplifted I can't even talk. I get this high vibration feeling in my heart. I almost feel like I'm flying. There could be absolutely no reason at all for this overwhelming feeling of joy. I just know I'm feeling it.

I think out of all the best ways I have learned to express my emotions, being in the car is my favorite. I have had personal concerts in my car. I embrace my emotions and submerge myself into music. I take the long way home so the feeling can last.

Also, when I'm listening to a story and it has a beautiful ending, I get chills. It's almost like I shared that emotion in the story. I feel just as happy as the person talking.

Our happiness is our own responsibility. Yes, it does help to have someone help you keep your vibration lifted, but not everyone has a person to help them. The future is unknown and when or if that person leaves or passes on to the next realm of being it would be so hard to learn how to heal yourself all over again.

It's important to learn that our happiness within ourselves. There's no class you can take to learn these gifts. We all have them. The free will we have is exactly that-- free. We have a free will to decide on our choices. This applies to our emotions as well.

You may ask, "What's Vibration? How do I get them higher?" It's really simple. We do it every day. It's another way of saying I had a positive attitude and expressed it vocally and physically by saying encouraging affirmations to ourselves, or by hugging ourselves, or both. Getting affirmations cards or writing one down daily also helps.

DIFFICULTY WITH INTIMACY

Ever feel the yearnings of intimacy that it starts to hurt your inside, and so deep that in your sleep reminiscing takes over, and it feels like you can almost touch it?

You know I really had to do some soul searching on this emotion. The more time I spent alone, the more I felt this yearning sensation. My body actually starts to ache. My abdomen feels like it's throbbing. Like it's missing something. I've had some vivid dreams of previous encounters I have experienced. I can almost smell the sweat, I can almost hear the sweet whispers and I can almost feel the fulfillment.

If you're anything like me and have some confusing perspectives of intimacy you would be questioning and analyzing everything about that dream. You ask yourself, "Was it wrong? Is it normal? Who can I talk to about this?" Shame and embarrassment take over and instead of learning about our bodies, we retreat back to the little cave we created for safety.

For a woman to reach out for a night of exchanging emotions is so wrong in some people's eyes. However, for a man to do it, he's honored. For a woman to dress provocatively she's seen as promiscuous, but for a man, he's trying to be a woman. For a woman to explore multiple partners, she's degraded and for a man, he's respected. No matter how you react to the yearning of your body, you're going to be judged for it. You might as well do what's going to make you happy -- of course within reason.

Don't let rejection get in the way of your evolving. There's really nothing to be ashamed of, nothing really to be embarrassed about. Free will is as free as it comes.

VULNERABILITY

Ever feel so vulnerable that waiting for someone to save you seemed worth the loss of time? You ever realize that you are that someone stuck pondering on accepting the burden of staying in limbo?

I felt so guilty of this behavior. Sometimes I just wanted to crawl into a ball and wait for someone to come and save me. I felt like I was drowning, and I needed a life jacket. I was in so much pain. I was willing to sit in it and pray for someone to come and help me. I believed the suffering was worth the wait until I was almost dead.

I was vulnerable that I was willing to settle for things I never would've if my mind was clear. So vulnerable until I was lost. So, lost that I patiently waited for someone to save me and when he came, I was vulnerable and believed it was real. I worked so many years for my person.

Loyalty and dedication are what I gave up in exchange for abundance and security. Sacrifices and persuasion were my gift. I should have known better. Maybe I did, but I didn't want to see it. Vulnerability signed away my livelihood.

One day I was so desperate for success, I even fell to my knees and offered my soul in exchange for fulfillment. I really didn't know what I was asking for until the knock on the door came for collection. One day I was thriving and moving forward and then the next day I was faced with an ultimatum. All these years I put into one place-my home. All of the emotions I surrendered to it. All of the mended fences that were created, where there, under that very special place. Then here I was having to choose to either have sex with the owner or move out. There was no in-between. I felt that I did what I could on my part to keep myself above water. I disciplined myself enough to know if I chose to have sex with this man, I was going to regret it for the rest of my life. He saw my vulnerability before I even acknowledged it. He waited for the right moment to strike. He was almost 30 years older than me. He knew I had no one and nothing else. My vulnerability was violated and taken advantage of in that moment.

I, in some way, manifested an ugly desire for an ugly deed and when I didn't follow through on my part. I lost everything. I lost it all. Once again, I had to face the world all alone. I brewed a poisonous spell and in return, I got a perversion outcome.

Exposing my vulnerability cost me the death of my own self. Yes, when we change, we have to die unto ourselves. It was one of the hardest, darkest and most confusing times of my life. I was so scared to be alone. I waited for the wrong person to save me. When I realized it, it was too late. He already had my life in his hands. It took everything out of me. I gave this place, his place, all of my mind, body and soul. For me to lose it all over sex was heartbreaking. It's been over 10 years and I still struggle with this experience. Sometimes I feel like I never left that nightmare. Triggers are everywhere.

It wasn't until I found my strength and purpose, that I was able to breathe again. I now have to wake up and consciously make the decision to be positive every single day. I now offer my soul in exchange for good deeds and hard-working abundance. I wake up and honor myself and accept who I am without anyone else's influences. I can look at myself in the mirror and say, "Self, you have come a long way. Walking away from abundance without a purpose was the best thing you could have done for yourself."

Vulnerability, it almost killed me. Both by being naive and vulnerable all together and by exposing my vulnerability to the wrong people.

LIFE AFTER DEATH

Ever sit in grief and it feels like the world is ending and life will never be the same? Do you ever ask, "Is all of the grief is real?"

Grief, it has to be one of the hardest emotions to discipline. Everyone reacts differently. Everyone processes grief differently. But man, when it hits your home, it really tears up everything and everyone with it. Especially if you're with an addict, you don't know what to expect. The sleepless nights are a real thing. The racing thoughts go 100 miles a minute. The unknown seems so much bigger. Unexplainably bigger. You start to ask yourself, "What happens after death? Does my family know I love them? Even the ones I am at odds with?"

My first relevant death was in 2003, my maternal grandma. She was really sick. She had a few things wrong with her. Battles she wasn't strong enough to fight. She made the conscious decision to surrender herself. We, as a family, stood by her side through her whole experience. I was fortunate enough to tell her the things I needed to tell her, to send her with so much love and support. Every Mother's Day will forever feel empty, every Christmas will not feel like home, every birthday I won't be able to bring her flowers. It has forever changed me. But not all experiences are beautiful, some are traumatic.

When my dad passed away in 2004, it was a traumatic experience. There was no warning, no options, no grace period no beautiful farewell. He was once here and then he wasn't. He loved heroin. He loved it so much it took his life. It robbed him of all his grandkids. All of the accomplishments of his kids and their kids. We were not on good terms when this happened. I sit with resentment and grief. I sit with confused feelings about boundaries and free will. As far as I know, there was nothing I could have done to change him, I wish I would've tried harder.

I know I'm not supposed to beat myself up over his mistakes, but as any passionate daughter would feel, I still do.

Grief can change our lives forever.

FINDING HOPE AT HOME

Ever go back to your childhood town and drive-by your old house?
You laugh at all the good memories and the sense of being home is

everything you remember it being.

I would have these dreams that I was back home in the house I grew up in as a child. In my dream I was living in the same house, but I was older. My family was still living their lives in this same place. The roses my dad planted were still fresh and the colors were still so vibrant. My childhood home was a place where you could drop your load off at the door and come in and be treated like family.

When things would get really confusing or overwhelming for me, I would have a tendency to retreat back to my childhood home. I feel safe there. If I couldn't physically get there, my spirit knew to astroplane there while I was sleeping. Before I even understood what that meant, my dreams would leave me feeling so much sadness from the loss of my grandmother. After having someone break down my dreams it was then that I started accepting her loss as a blessing rather than as a selfish feeling I was having. It almost feels conflicting.

You want them to pass on and you want to be happy knowing there was no more suffering for them. At the same time, you want to grab them out of your dream and physically bring them home. When I would have these dreams, I usually woke up angry at the Universe for taking my loved one away because I was being selfish because I wanted them back. I had to mentally discipline my emotions and remind myself that my loved one's time was up and now they needed to move on to the next realm.

Recently I drove myself back to my childhood home and it was like I had a Deja vu. I mean from second to second it felt like I was traveling back in time. That day I was told to use some rose oil and it would do something magical for me. I of course did and let me tell you, that weekend we drove through town, the Universe showed me everything I needed to see. It was so beautiful and fulfilling. I walked outside early in the morning at about 8 AM. The air smelled like wet grass. The fog was heavy. The elementary school, Westfield Elementary, still had the same playground equipment. I was home.

I desperately wanted to stay behind and pick up from where I left off. Where I was in cheerleading. When school was my everyday routine. Where the stars are brighter, and the air is cleaner. Where I met love for the first time. Where my grandma would make tamales on the kitchen table whistling to the Spanish music in the background. Meanwhile, grandpa would be outside in the backyard fixing something, anything. Where the swing set and trapeze bar grandpa made me hung on the biggest trees I have ever seen for a backyard. Where I got my hand smacked for trying to make my grandma a grilled cheese sandwich. I was so excited to show her I could cook. Grandpa was not having it. He said, "No, you don't touch the stove that's what I'm here for, I will cook for you." A lot of my important childhood firsts live in Porterville, California.

When we went to visit, my mom and I sat and took pictures across the street like weirdos and just laughed at all the fun times we had there. All that love generated from one little woman.

Sometimes in life retreating back to a place that makes us feel safe is so important. It will do a few things for you. It will definitely humble you. It will even show you you're altered past and what could have been. It will show you what you no longer are. It can even make you feel like you don't even know who that person was. It will make you see all your growth.

Taking that drive, visiting my old home and running into old friends has definitely humbled me. It has also motivated me to expand my perspectives and at the same time, it took away all my pain and disconnection. It reminded me that I'm someone's daughter, I'm someone's mother and I'm someone's friend. Even though my purpose hasn't yet exposed itself, I know it's there.

DEPRESSION AT DEATH'S DOOR

Ever spend so much time alone death seemed but a reach
away? It's seems like you can almost see it. It's feels like
you can reach out and touch it, but it disappears because

it's not your time.

Depression feels just like that and it's harder on someone
when they're alone. The best way to explain this is when
you're spending so much time alone you start thinking
you don't matter. When you have a mental condition it
just intensives the emotions. Sometimes the emotions are
so dark and painful death seems so much easier. It feels
like a sudden rush of all negative energies take over your
mind. Every single thought hurts and all the traumatic
flashbacks that knock you to your knees. There's no one
there to intervene. No one there to rub your head or give
you the affirmations you need to hang onto. No one to

make sure the that thoughts of death don't take over you.

I don't care how good your life is right now, all of us have met this emotion. Not everyone can climb out of it. Not everyone can handle the trauma, some never recover. It took me over 10 years to get my head together and strong enough to understand how important it is to forgive others. Forgiveness is for my own sanity. Even if they aren't sorry. I'm strong enough now to discipline my emotions. I know better. I know that I am who I am because of all the ugly things I went through. I have built my strength in all these accomplishments. I know it's okay to feel all these somber feelings, but I couldn't stay there.

I'm strong enough to know that sitting in my sorrow wasn't going to move me. There wasn't anyone coming to save me. No knight in shining armor. I eventually had to get my ass up and start over. As for death, we don't even realize how close we are to it every single day. How we are one mistake away from meeting it. I find comfort in accepting and embracing death. It becomes a celebration rather than a loss. The hurt isn't as heavy, and I made a new friend.

SADNESS MIXED WITH LONELY IS A BAD COMBINATION

Ever wake up with so much sadness that you wish you never woke up? You feel like your sense of purpose is so far away.

I remember the first day after I was fired from the place, I mentioned in chapter 10. I was so sad. I was no longer part of what I thought was my purpose. I was so confused. I went into shock. I lost 50 pounds from malnutrition and vomiting from being so embarrassed. I woke up with an ache in my heart.

The emotion I felt is almost similar to the death of a loved one. I didn't know who I was, where I was going, I slept for days. I had this same reaction from when my loved ones passed away. Except being sad and confused was now my reality every day. I will forever feel a deep sadness when I drive by that place.

That person who I was then had to die unto herself. Sounds weird, I know, but I literally had to forget everything I ever knew and learn how to reprogram my thought process and my habits. My faith simplified my lifestyle.

Break up and sadness can also push your thoughts to this breaking point. Losing someone and waking up the very next day to no one can be scary. It's like your sense of purpose was just lost. One day you're planning your future and the next you wake up sad and alone. Death seems lighter than the alone feeling. Death seems so close but so far away. It's almost teasing you.

Lonely sadness hurts deep.

IMPULSIVE DECISIONS

Ever make an impulsive decision and you know better, but every
excuse seems so valid? Giving in was the only way to fill the void.

Impulsive decisions should be my middle name. I used
to be intrigued by cutting myself. It was never too deep
but deep enough to release this imaginary steam. Almost
like smoke coming out of my pores. Every time I did it
the more, I wanted to do it and the deeper I would go.
Then I discovered tattoos. I mean I've been around people with them my whole life, but tattoos didn't spark my
interest until I started self-harming. Needless to say, I
have tattoos everywhere. I don't see an ending to that yet.
Most of the tattoos I have are impulsive decisions.

Shopping online is also an impulsive decision of mine.

It seems like when I have a little extra money, I want to hit the "Buy now" button. Not so much because I need something, but because I want to keep the numbers in my account at a certain amount. Strange? Yes, I know but this is definitely normal for an impulsive thinker. You would think letting my coins build-up would be smarter and I totally agree but my impulsivity won't allow that to happen.

I notice when I get out of the car, I look in my purse like three times. I dust off the dashboard and I check the door. When I'm done with this, I repeat the same thing until I hear that voice in my head that says get out. Sometimes before I leave the house, I walk around my room a couple of times to check my nightstand, touch my dresser and overlook my desk for nothing. I'm literally looking for nothing. And once I've done this a few times and I feel like there's nothing I'm missing then I move on to the next thing I need to do.

GROWING IN JAIL

Ever sit in a jail cell where the cold is colder, and the hurt is hurting but it taught you acceptance of others?

I remember the first time I sat in a real jail cell. I was so flustered, and nerve wrecked. I was arrested under false pretenses and held for almost a week in Lynwood, California. Charges were never filed. No case was ever made. Hell, I didn't even make it into the courtroom. I think they even forgot about me when they did a court call. I had to ask if my name was even on the list.

But I'll tell you what it did do. It introduced me to the hurting, to the despair, and to survival. It taught me how to accept people for who they are. It taught me how to love a little extra. How to reach out in a universal language. How to make an effort to have a better understanding. It forced me to talk to strangers and share my background. It was definitely out of my comfort zone.

Using the bathroom in front of others is so awkward. Especially if you have never had to do that before. Watching someone else use the restroom in front of you is even more awkward. It's like do I stare. Do I turn around? The grouping of each other was so uncomfortable. Yet there's women who do this on a daily basis. There's women who get up every cold morning with no fluffy blanket or soft pillow to lay on. There's women who don't have a loved one to say good night to every night. There's women who get up and survive the best way they know-how.

I got to see all of that up close and personal. It humbled me in a way I cannot explain. Even though it was a mistake me ending up there, it was also a blessing of knowledge and building of character.

MIRROR MIRROR ON THE WALL

Ever stare in the mirror and you ask your reflection "Who are you?"
Waiting for a sign, a blink, or a delayed expression to find out the
answer ends up bigger than you.

I realized the mysteries of life will not reveal itself without the sacrifices it requires. We can stare as long as we want, and nothing will happen. You will just start to analyze all your flaws. You will get nervous because of all the urban legends that we grew up hearing. Unless of course, if you're into other realms of mirror magic.

You watch these scary movies, or these fairy tales and all these things magically happen. Would it be weird to actually try it? One day I literally stood in front of the mirror and waited for a blink I didn't do or a delayed smile.

Then I started panicking wondering what if that really did happen. I probably would run out of the room.

The only thing it did for me was make me notice all my imperfections. I started to feel more insecure about my features. I also started imagining changes to my face. I admire women who can take their time in the mirror and do their makeup. The ones who pull out their compacts to freshen up. It's never really been up my alley. One time I had my makeup done and I instantly wanted to wash my face off. My face felt so heavy. Then one day I decided to take a few minutes out of my day and look in the mirror and accept all of my imperfections, freshen up and continue my day.

Baby steps will always lead to bigger steps.

NINE LIVES

Ever feel like you've lived more than one lifetime, yet you're still living your lifetime even though it doesn't seem like a lifetime?

Talk about confusing thoughts. It honestly feels like I have lived a few lifetimes. Each lifetime served a purpose. I'm not afraid to say I've tried different ways of living. I did it mostly for what I thought was best for my kids and I at that time. Raising four kids, two boys and two girls, was not easy. The majority of the time it was my responsibility to be both parents. I had no clue on how to raise boys to men.

Each serious relationship I have had was a different type of lifestyle. Each one also had the same outcome. Me, having to create boundaries that would lead to a divorce or a separation. I have no regrets. Each lifetime started with the butterflies in the stomach. At one time there was a connection. I have learned so much from each partner. I'm also grateful for the mourning feelings at the end of each lifetime. It built character in me.

It took me 42 years to finally understand that we do live in different lifetimes in our one life. We live in different decades, through different trends, and with different partners. All of these changes take place.

I do believe we meet people in our lives for a reason and sometimes those reasons we mess up because of our own toxic ways. For example, maybe someone came into our lives to teach us how to evolve and instead you fall in love with them and end up in a relationship. A relationship that was only meant to be taught how to evolve but now you're emotionally wrapped up in that person's chaos rather than growing and evolving. Or you end up meeting someone and you automatically connect. That person becomes your best friend, and you end up getting into an argument and stop being friends because of our own toxic habits. Instead of learning and growing together as friends, we end up with grudges and animosity. How do we know who's who?

Learning about self-evolution is usually not taught in school. Intuition is not something that is usually taught in our homes. Self-healing and meditation are usually not shown to us at a young age. In life, most of us stumble on this knowledge and when we do it becomes our responsibility to learn it and teach it to our kids.

I know that thinking about how we live different lives in our one lifetime can be so mind-blowing. When you hit this phase, you will know. It's like an epiphany. You will wake up each lifetime and know if it's time to change or it's time to start something else.

When I think about this gift we were given. It's a reminder to me that out of all my life and after all my trials and tribulations, I'm still living and breathing but in a different place, a different mindset, wearing different clothes, with a different body shape, and I can still start over in whatever life I'm living.

How powerful. If we could've just grasped this concept a little earlier, it could've stopped so many heartbreaks and wasted time. We could be successful. We wouldn't beat each other up. We would be better supporters. Family grudges would be repairable.

I do my best to live each lifetime with grace, honor, and empowerment.

SAY, "CHEESE!"

Ever feel so beautiful, you snap a picture of the moment trying to capture the feeling, but all anyone else can see is a photo?

Selfies are the new evolution. When we feel confident these days, we take a selfie- a picture of ourselves. We could even use filters to either enhance our features or make us look silly. We post it for the world to see or for our friends and family. We want to show them we are doing good. We feel good.

What they don't see are all the battle wounds we had to endure to get there. The tears we wiped before that beautiful selfie. The pieces of our hearts that we had to glue back together so we can face the world through a simple photo. The pats on our backs that we had to do on our

own and mind you we can barely even reach our own
backs.

If you're anything like me, you're very shy and self-con-
scious. It takes about 10 pictures to get one that is semi-
cute. It takes several times turning around into different
lighting areas in your room. Then once you share the picture, you want to cover your eyes. You even throw the
phone and say a quick prayer, "People be nice."

Not that it matters what people think. It's just you know
what it took to get you strong enough to get to that con-
fidence level. You remember all the doubts you had to
push away. All the critics you had to stand up against just
so you can feel balanced.

We are all uniquely made. A picture doesn't capture an
emotion, but what it does do is capture the memory of
that emotion through your smile. Through your captions
that are sent out to the world. Try to take as many as you
can. Also compliment someone else's photo. Spread your
vibration out to someone else who may desperately need
it.

RESPECTING THE MOON

Ever cry to the moon? Arms out spinning like a child wishing on the
stars, praying to the unknown.

I try to do this monthly and especially on a full moon. I
normally say a prayer. I pretty much make up my own.
I mostly go with what I feel in my heart and what feels
right in my gut.

Our intuition- the solar plexus chakra. If you're balanced
and you've been studying self-care you would understand
what our solar plexus chakra is to our body. It is yellow
and located below our chest. It carries our self-power and
personal responsibilities. So whatever we feel that may
disturb our self-values or morality we tend to shy away
from it, Trust that feeling.

I always keep this in mind when I write my own prayers.

When I present my dreams and wishes to the full moon, it gives me an overwhelming sense of security. I start to feel light. My eyes fill up with tears of mourning and joy from new beginnings. It becomes conflicting sometimes, so I have to remember to discipline my emotions and take in one at a time.

The follow-through of this action is so important. Just like anything else, we have to do our part. Once we present ourselves to the moon, things will start to change around us. This is when our practice of disciplining ourselves comes into play. It is so important that we stay focused on what it is we cried to the moon for our lives or our current situations.

Relationships will fall apart. New relationships will form. We will lose a job, or we will have a new opportunity for a different job. We will lose our best friend, but we will also gain one. Anyone that is negative or toxic in our lives will be disturbed around your presence and you will notice but at the same time all those that have a higher purpose will wrap their arms around you.

I cry out to the Universe.

In my belief, the Universe is everyone's belief in one while respecting nature and the mysterious gifts we possess as spiritual beings. When crying out to the moon is not to be taken lightly because it will answer.

BRAVE

Ever just put all your guards down, exposing yourself to another person? You risk your vulnerabile state of mind by searching for support.

Sometimes during our vulnerability phase, we seem to let our guard down. All the boundaries we built over our pain. If we are brave enough, we will even let people see us cry.

Unfortunately for us, we have to face all these emotions that hurt us or experiences that have forever changed us. Death, divorce, birth, any life-changing experiences that have left us with somber feelings. For us to be able to completely work through these emotions and not feel them anymore we have to let our guard down. We have to find a trusted friend, family member, or an outside outlet to bounce perspectives with.

I remember one time I called our family healer, Lily Therese, and I vented to her about a personal dilemma and her response was, "Have you told anyone else how you're feeling? Have you talked to others outside the home?" Of course, I didn't I was too embarrassed. I was embarrassed for so long, I didn't realize how far I let things slip away. Once I started opening up to a few trusted friends and hearing their experiences, it really put things into perspective for me.

I would take everyone's trials and errors into consideration and use the best outcomes and put them together and make my own decisions. You pretty much know what you need to do to change or what you need to let go of to get a better outcome. We can feel it. Nonetheless hearing confirmations from people that have shared your experiences is helpful.

Sometimes it's necessary to let our guard down. Just think about it like this. Is it worth the risk? If your gut is weighing more on yes, just go with it, but if your gut is saying no, and you will know because you will want to vomit, then the answer is no- go with it.

We will really never know who we can and can't trust when we let our guard down. We just have to do it.

THE WEIGHT OF THE PRESSURE

Ever feel so much pressure your head feels like it
can literally explode?

There's so much pressure on us these days. We have to have some kind of side hustle to be able to feed our families. If you're anything like me, your family has to come together and split the rent. Most of the time the pressure gets built up so much you literally feel like you're going to explode. It's a real emotion. Sometimes we don't even realize it's happening until we've had a mental breakdown. Even the strongest of the strong have breakdowns.

We've taken our self-image to extremes where we put so much pressure on ourselves to be perfect. We even have surgery. We allow doctors that we don't even know to open us up and stick foreign objects in our bodies just so we can feel good. When in reality all that ends up happening is you will find something else wrong and you will want to change that.

The pressure of our self-image is so influential by the media. We all want to look like we are in our prime. Happy, glowing and ambitious. It has such an impact on how we feel about ourselves when we look in the mirror. We see these commercials or reality tv shows. You see when the reality tv cast starts from episode one to the season finale how they have changed dramatically. From looking like us average people to looking perfect. Granted these beautiful people have to change their lifestyles to maintain their appearance so the sacrifice is real. But the pressure for us non-celebrity status people builds as we see how much money we have to hustle to be able to afford such a miracle. The pressure builds so much that we start to put liens on our houses or take loans out of our retirement funds just to attempt to let some of this pressure go.

It took me 42 years to be able to pinpoint my pressure triggers. This is absolutely one of them. I've had four children all-natural births all at a young age and all breastfed. If you're a mom, you definitely know what a baby can do to your body. There are days I don't even want to look at myself in the mirror.

What I have learned after sorting through all these emotions is that if I give myself some patience and put in the work that is necessary to get to where I want to be, the pressure is lighter. I also noticed if I start telling myself that I'm fine the way I am and no one can change my opinion about myself, the pressure lessens.

I woke up one day and just decided that I was going to look in the mirror everyday and say. "Self, you made it this far!"

WE ARE NOT WORTHY

Ever been so thankful you fall to your knees humbly recognizing you are not worthy feeling guilty and you accept all the grace we are given?

I have come to the point in my life where I feel so thankful. I wake up thankful, and I go to bed thankful. I am even thankful for all my bad karma. I feel thankful for the struggles I had to endure. I am thankful for all the accomplishments I had to reach. I'm thankful for the grieving of my own selfishness. When I break everything down that I'm thankful for it gives me this overwhelming sense of humbleness.

I feel so humbled that it takes me to my knees. Literally, I will drop to my knees. This happens most of the time when I'm in the shower. I feel the most humbleness when I'm naked. I feel so exposed to the world. I begin to wash my body with soap from the face down to my toes and while I'm doing this, I'm whispering to the Universe, "Wash away anything that is not of my highest good and replace it with everything that is meant for me. I accept my life's purpose. I am light and love." I do this until I feel like I've washed all my faults away and any negative thoughts or words sent my way. I do this until I start feeling lighter.

If you close your eyes you will start to see colors. Purples, blues, even geometric shapes or shapes that you can't even make out. That's all normal. I started doing some research on the process of aligning your chakras and I'm finding the same answers. It's all normal. If you're anything like me and already have experienced this stage then you'll know when I say be careful while trying this because you could be so deep in yourself that your spirit is actually being lifted and when you open your eyes too fast you can feel off-balanced and fall.

I look at my kids and I'm thankful all over again. To be

able to be a mother of these specific spirits, I am honored. Watching them find their way, I am thankful I'm here to be able to see it and to be a part of it.

Ever since I grasped the basic fundamentals of self-healing and self-love, I was able to make the changes necessary to break my generational curses and karma. To be able to pass on knowledge of what I know is true and teach my loved ones who will teach their loved ones. These fundamentals of life, our lives, are so important to learn. Always be thankful.

I discovered as long as we keep feeding ourselves with positive affirmations, we will continue to see positive outcomes. As long as we make it a point to look in the mirror once a day. Even knowing that after all our ugliness we are still given grace. I acknowledge that none of us are worthy of the grace we are given; I still smile with thankfulness.

If I were to die tomorrow, know this, I loved being a young mother, I did the best I could with what I had, I followed and depended on all my intuition. I made every effort to pass on knowledge from experiences, especially if it could change someone's life. I will always be thankful for all the lifetimes I have been blessed to live.

SPECIAL
ACKNOWLEDGEMENTS TO

The Universe, for everything above and everything below.

My Daughters, Korina and Ines.

My Sons, Baby David and Martin.

My Grandparents, Senovia and Magdaleno Baltazar.

My Parents, Sylvia and Fabian Trebizo.

My Husband and the father of my children, Big D.

My Mother in Law, Nancy Clifford.

My Brother In Law, Alex (Rest In Peace).

My Spirit Guides, Lily Therese and Sandyi Offermann.

My Graphic Design Rick Garcia

My Partners, Christina Cummings and Arilia Winn.

My Publisher, Winn Publications LLC.

ABOUT THE AUTHOR

Fabrienne "Fabs" Trebizo was born on August 29, 1977. She has written a manuscript about her childhood and how she was able to break the cycle. In the manuscript, she talks about how she was able to deal with obstacles that some never overcome. Suffering from a heroin-addicted father who tremendously abused her mother, Fabs witnessed this abuse as if it was an everyday routine. However, because of her circumstances she suffered so much pain and agony and tried to commit suicide.

Instead of learning from the terrible experiences, she started following the same cycle that she saw at her home. She ended up with the same kind of abusive relationships as a young woman. And just when she thought she was getting it together, two of the most influential people of her life passed away in a years time. Her turning point was when she acknowledged that her life wasn't going anywhere and she was suffering deep inside. For the love of her children, she decided to leave her old self, the Fabs that she was accustomed to, and broke the cycle!

Fab's educational background is in the Early Childhood Development Field. For 11 years she was an Executive Director at a Learning Facility where she worked with a diverse range of families and children from the ages of six weeks to 12 years old.

In 2011, Fabs was diagnosed with PTSD due to a traumatic experience at the workplace and decided to formulate a Non-Profit Organization that reaches families with such issues and helps change the thinking process of the youth at risk. Since 2013, she has successfully launched Coexist 13, an organization geared towards the youth. Coexist 13 has since successfully networked with an amazing group of people.

VISIT US ON THE WEB!

SIGN UP FOR NEWS + UPDATES

Be the first to know about:

Events
Giveaways
Discounts
and so much more!

Sign up at allofus.shop now!

SUPPORT THIS AUTHOR AND LEAVE A REVIEW.

Sammy,
It has been a
pleasure getting to
know you and work with
you throughout our
life times

Love You,
Gabrienne

Made in the USA
Middletown, DE
27 July 2020